ELEPHants TRUMPet!

Pam Scheunemann

Consulting Editor, Diane Craig, M.A./Reading Specialist

A Division of ABDO

ABDO
Publishing Company

visit us at www.abdopublishing.com

Published by ABDO Publishing Company, a division of ABDO, P.O. Box 398166, Minneapolis, Minnesota 55439. Copyright © 2011 by Abdo Consulting Group, Inc. International copyrights reserved in all countries. No part of this book may be reproduced in any form without written permission from the publisher. SandCastle™ is a trademark and logo of ABDO Publishing Company.

Printed in the United States of America, North Mankato, Minnesota
102010
012011

Editor: Liz Salzmann
Content Developer: Nancy Tuminelly
Cover and Interior Design and Production: Oona Gaarder-Juntti, Mighty Media, Inc.
Photo Credits: Shutterstock

Library of Congress Cataloging-in-Publication Data
Scheunemann, Pam, 1955-
  Elephants trumpet! / Pam Scheunemann.
    p. cm. -- (Animal sounds)
  ISBN 978-1-61613-571-3
  1. Elephants--Vocalization--Juvenile literature. I. Title.
  QL737.P98S334 2011
  599.67'1594--dc22
                              2010018750

SandCastle™ Level: Transitional

SandCastle™ books are created by a team of professional educators, reading specialists, and content developers around five essential components—phonemic awareness, phonics, vocabulary, text comprehension, and fluency—to assist young readers as they develop reading skills and strategies and increase their general knowledge. All books are written, reviewed, and leveled for guided reading, early reading intervention, and Accelerated Reader® programs for use in shared, guided, and independent reading and writing activities to support a balanced approach to literacy instruction. The SandCastle™ series has four levels that correspond to early literacy development. The levels are provided to help teachers and parents select appropriate books for young readers.

Emerging Readers	Beginning Readers	Transitional Readers	Fluent Readers
(no flags)	(1 flag)	(2 flags)	(3 flags)

Contents

ELEPHANTS

The elephant is the biggest animal around.

It can make a loud trumpeting sound.

Trumpeting is not the only sound elephants make. They can also bark, growl, and snort.

Elephants live in groups called herds.

Females of all ages and young males live in a herd. Adult males live alone or in small groups.

They greet each
other without words.

Elephants often touch each other's trunks as a greeting. It's like they are shaking hands.

One thing they like to do is eat.

Elephants eat up to 300 pounds (136 kg) of food each day!

You can tell they are big just by their feet!

An elephant's feet have thick pads of fat under the skin. They help hold the elephant's weight.

An elephant's trunk is like a long nose.

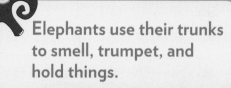

Elephants use their trunks to smell, trumpet, and hold things.

It can also be used like a garden hose!

An elephant can suck water into its trunk. It can spray the water, or put it in its mouth to drink.

Elephants use their sense of smell to tell when there is danger.

An elephant can sense when danger is near.

It trumpets a warning loud and clear.

Elephants will trumpet if they are surprised or scared.

Once the danger has gone away, the elephants know that it's safe to play!

Elephants make rumbling sounds that only other elephants can hear. These noises tell the others that things are okay.

Glossary

female (p. 7) – being of the sex that can produce eggs or give birth. Mothers are female.

greet (p. 8) – to say or do something welcoming when you meet someone.

greeting (p. 9) – something welcoming that you say or do when you meet someone.

growl (p. 4) – to make a deep, low, threatening sound.

male (p. 7) – being of the sex that can father offspring. Fathers are male.

snort (p. 4) – to make a short, loud noise by breathing out suddenly through the nose.

warning (p. 20) – a sound or message that means something bad could happen.

Elephant Around the World

English - elephant

French - éléphant

Hindi - hathi

Japanese - zo

Russian - slon

Spanish - elefante